Speed of Life

Edward Kleinschmidt Mayes

Apogee Press
Berkeley · California
1999

and again, for Frances

A great deal of thanks goes to the editors of the following journals in which poems from this book, some in earlier versions, were first published:

The Alembic: "No" and "War" (as "Triage")
American Letters & Commentary: "Birth" (as "*De Die Natali*")
Colorado Review: "Sudden"
Epoch: "Okeydokey"
Fine Madness: "Equal Sign"
The Greensboro Review: "Brisance"
Gulf Coast: "Hang Man" and "Synapse"
Indiana Review: "*Subito*"
The Journal: "The Beginning of the Last Fall" (as "31 August 1986")
New American Writing: "*Après Débris*"
New England Review: "Violence" (as "Kill Or Be Killed") and "To Remain"
Passages North: "Preoccupation"
Poetry East: "Abortion," "Capital Punishment," "Nuclear War,"
    "Racism, Classism, Sexism," and "Welfare Reform"
Southwest Review: "No for an Answer"
Tampa Review: "Chances and Hazards"
Three Rivers Poetry Journal: "Rapid Fire"
Witness: "Humiliation" and "Speed of Life"

"Blood Bank" appeared in *Elvis in Oz: New Stories and Poems from the Hollins Creative Writing Program* (University Press of Virginia)

"To Remain" was first published by The Heyeck Press in its Flowering Quince Poetry Series. The poem was reprinted in *Best of New England Review: The Readers' Issue.*

Thanks go to Santa Clara University for release time and a Thomas Terry Award, both of which aided me in finishing this manuscript, and to the Virginia Center for the Creative Arts and The MacDowell Colony, where some of this collection was written.

Book design by Philip Krayna. Cover photograph ©1999 Philip Krayna.

ISBN 0-9669937-0-5. Library of Congress Catalog Card Number 99-072276.

Published by Apogee Press, Post Office Box 8177, Berkely CA, 94707-8177.

Table of Contents

· Prologue ·

Sudden

Death rolls its baby buggy onto the tollway and the cars
scream and honk in delight. It's breakfast in America—
the snap crackle pop of bones breaking, heads whacked,
good blood starting to flow. The good will won't. We have
all been so suddenly happy, so suddenly sad, standing
in the line for extreme unction when we should be
rioting in this life, uncivil servants, dangerous children.
I've been strip searched—nothing found. I could rub
the skin off my entire body and find nothing underneath,
nothing to be cast, no lost wax techniques to rediscover.
Who'll give the final boot to the Heil Hitler? Kids in
my neighborhood goosestep off to college, hearts clogged
with black blood. We once needed the past. Ask anyone.
Blunt talk about crib death. Infant gangs. Teenagers
pump up their bike tires until everything explodes, including
adults, insurance premiums, save-the-world slogans,
toboggan parties, the church steak-fry, Polish jokes, manholes.
We've been looking for the typewriter with the keys that
would pound out *Wait a minute*. I have
not wasted my life by taking out the trash. It all
happened so suddenly. But no, really. I enjoy
the buildup. I'm not of two minds. Climax is
the ladder with wonderful rungs. We simply
start singing. Do I not want to go this way, not
in the 2000 car pile up on the last freeway known
to mankind? I want my main arteries to ignite,
flash flood of blood, some spiritual cyclone,
taking me, taking me up, taking me up, taking me.

· One ·

Birth

Some small eruption could shake this small house
down, pull the common nails out, splinter all the board
feet into taller trees again, to make up for all the time
they spent being what held up this house. The constellations
each night are beyond me. Instead, those steadfast stars
are falling, have fallen too fast to be seen. I want to rip
the sky in half, but I obviously can't. I want to foretell
disasters from the flight patterns of birds, but I can't.
And I can't not, this world having been born so quietly
one day, a day I've never known, can't know. Why the word
birth at all? At times, time. At other times, the space
around time that closes in on it. The sands from
the hourglass filter through the hands of the wall clock.
The time we are having, that we've had. The time
in the pocket of the blue jeans. The time in the desk
drawer. And day, the sweet buffoon who stays too long after
dinner, but we've never seemed to mind much. He had some
good stories he told over and over. About the round the world
train trip. The car ride to eternity. How for seven years
Calypso kept him from his own apocalypse. We were born
like all the rest, like rust that makes the piece of iron
unusable. Who will use the least life, hand us the last
ladle of cool water? It's a day we forgot to remember to
forget to remember to forget. The big beget. The terror
of this earth moving, fist wanting to shatter the windows
that are our eyes. We got what we saw, but we couldn't quite
see it. But it was here all along, dying too fast to be
noticed, being born so quickly that the world had no response.
Not even breath breath breath can convince us we are still alive.

Chances and Hazards

The Theory of Falling Bodies has been proven.
But where else would they go if not down. As if
there were anything truly original about original
sin. There is a pair of dice in the world that
gamblers would die for. They roll each new pair
in their hands, white bones with black dots, and
blow for no accident in their luck. The sun
falls into the west at the end of each day,
accurately. Now it is getting darker
earlier. Nothing is as certain as the sun.
That's why there's no bet against its
rising, where east meets west, since the day
before we were born. I take a chance
when I believe that the Etruscans studied
the intestines of animals to tell the future.
The future is always the last thing we want
to know. What is to be done with the future?
There is always doubt to believe in, always
the letter bomb in the mailroom, always
the permanent crosshatching on the faces of criminals.

Hour

It was as if too many days had gone by,
too many of them beginning with the usual no,
the no's that at most take us to the corner

drugstore and maybe back. Now and at
the hour of our death I remember saying and
then remember forgetting for twenty years.

How does one get from forget to forgive? What
is the hard way? How does one wash one's hands
of something? We haven't any tally of the number

of ring fingers thieves cut off for rings. How
does one report a crime that happens so quickly,
the ten second this or that? Probably *for crime's*

sake isn't the right saying I've said many times,
but *for crying out loud* is, even though I'm not
sure what the subject and verb of the phrase

could be. But let's be straightforward—the plumb
bob is waiting for gravity to do its thing.
Okay, let's say you hit the nail on the head—

then what? Poetry is a good cure for inaccuracy.
At the hour of my death I will have written my
last line. Then I'll queue up to God and all

will be forgotten. The apple falls in its own
time. Or the hand grabs the cool curves and
picks it, like sex. I've never believed in

the drumroll. I don't have a minute to spare,
much less sixty. Why would anyone anymore want
to open a can of worms? My back space is broken,

so I have no choice but to go forward. Saying yes
can be a good experience. How many hours are there
now in each day? The countdown, the letup,

the comeback—we've had our days, long silvery ones,
like the backs of the olive leaves, and the wood that
burns long and bright until it is overcome by its own ash.

No for an Answer

The question is yes, as if you're
walking in the door and you hear
yes, and you yourself are not
any answer to which anybody would swear.
There are odd and there are even people.
You've thrown stones in the noctiluca
and watched the phosphorescence ripple.
You've been living at the no-fault line
for years. You drop your n's on *nevers*,
affix them to *evers*. If there's no
one at noon to have lunch with, the noon
whistle will still blow, and you can eat in quiet,
in *non sequitur*. This time will be,
at most, semi-eternal. And you can't
negotiate for more. The ghosts around
your bed are singing *noli me tangere*,
but you wouldn't if you could and you
couldn't. You pitched a no-hitter
in your sleep one bright Saturday afternoon.
No words were opposed to yes. Think now, think
now, think now. How is it that the hat is on
the hat stand? Yes? The final guess at
the crossword puzzle? Another yes? The guest
who was a no-show at the baseball stadium where
the opera didn't quite work, was rained out?
If there could be anything as final as yes.
But not to worry about these questions. They give
the shape to your Sundays. Should you
have your cat neither neutered nor spayed?

There are mostly noes. Lake No is the source
of the White Nile, and you don't deny the sound
of the water rushing and falling. It gets better.
It all gets better. Is there no annulment for what
is null, for neglect, for half-lives, for annihilation?

Hang Man

The pencil lead pokes his eyes out,
no hood slipped over his head. Is
there an open vowel sound in *l, i, f, e,*
no wife grieving no doubt, since
we've invented him in this religion
class, all of us divided into small
groups to discuss sin? We swear it's
a sin to cuss, then move on to hang
this man, his life held by the right
guess of one of twenty-six
letters! Nail that sucker, the big
boys shout when they stone
the retard during recess. Would that
I could stop them, slapshot their
foreheads with a sixty miles-per-hour
hockey puck to shut them the fuck up.
O Lazarus—you look like the stickman
we draw and kill. I can't stay for
the execution. I've got no stomach
for the free fall to hell. And we'll
never guess the longest longest word,
every right letter, every consonant
of the blank death, every sound the trap
door makes, but will just watch every
slash that signifies an arm or a leg added
to a body we all know is beyond being saved.

Okeydokey

That is, the nozzle on the yes hose
is wide open, the verbs in complete
agreement with their subjects. The sound
of an oil can lubricating an opera hat.
It's stuck. What is its *modus
operandi*? People are nodding off
at the rest home. They belong to the chain
reaction. My father has diptych written
all over him, married now fifty years.
Ears were made for hearing. I wear chain
mail when I open the letter bombs. I
can't fiddle with victory. Where have
all the yes-men gone? The dingus turned
into a doo-hickey. It's just my luck.
Where is the son of a gun? The X
in X-mas? I will eclipse myself one
morning, clipping the hedges, disengaging
the claptrap, resetting the short circuit,
widening the narrow writing, keeping here today
here today, picturing yes yes yes yes yes orbiting no.

No

you who have smashed out your cigarette into my face
    you who have cut off my writing arm
you who have made all the hairs on my body
    reverse their directions
you who have destroyed a few last things I thought
    weren't worth destroying–

a fabulous jar of urine, moss from a favorite tree
    in my childhood, my father's fingerprints
on the kitchen doorknob
    you who have erased my eyebrows, put x's
where my eyes were, an imperfect circle for my mouth

    you who have thrown the bone bag on the pile of rock
you who have said that if gods weren't dead
    we'd have to kill them
you who have hollowed out wombs
    you who have booed at angels no one can see
you who have inherited the map with directions to hell

    you who have worn the latest news, the blizzard
of hate, the hurricane of hurt
    you who have unfurled the sheet I was buried in
and use it as a flag
    you who have chopped thought to the bone
then chopped the bone

    you who have harmed, have armies of harm,
who have the last words of everyone memorized, who live
    to die, who die for nothing and the nothing lasts,
who sell the trinkets of time for the trinkets of space,
    who hath not wrath nor meaning, who doth not
think of legs

tangled with other legs in quarry pits, head
with eyes jellied, hands with fingers uncrossed, minds
    no longer carrying what could and what could have
and what did not extinguish you

Synapse

I dreamt the plate of nerves was passed to me
I dreamt that every chance deserved a chance
I dreamt the ordinary life, the open book
I dreamt the hospital again, the windows broken out

You dreamt the writer going blind, the field of goats
You dreamt the razor going dull, the cold face
You dreamt the fire going out, the empty chair
You dreamt the feeling going dry, the rhubarb picked

Another shot at immortality today, I dreamt
Another time that seems to be the same, I dreamt
Another being I would love to forget, I dreamt
Another sun that doesn't deserve to set, I dreamt

The leaping cow, uneven surface of the moon, you dreamt
The colliding stars, the astronomical me, you dreamt
The cold getting colder, the colder getting colder, you dreamt
The erasing mind, the road crowded with cars, you dreamt

I dreamt the building all on fire, the fire out
You dreamt the same, the dendrites failing you
Another impulse gone, the axon dead, I dreamt
Another neuron dead, the impulse gone, you dreamt

Another dream you dreamt a dream you dreamt you dreamt
Another night of dream another dream you dreamt I dreamt

Après Débris

It's not that we haven't tried detritus,
        and it's not that we didn't like the look
of ruins, or the ruins of ruins, or the ruins
        of ruins of ruins. But there are ceilings
in our lives and there are false ceilings.
        I've too been witness to the big teardown,
the breakup and breakdown, the downtown
        and uptown artifacts fucked over. Holy
debris, rain down upon the motor mouths
        in the motor homes. Wire down
the accelerators for a lovely crash
        into a lovely wall. I'm thinking, *loose lips
sink*..., I'm thinking, *bury the*..., I'm thinking,
        after the fall...the great climb into a warm bed
to wait for spring! Something in place of
        smashed plates. Something moving, a small child
asleep in the back seat, and the car stopped
        in traffic. I'd rather go than stop or be gone.
I'd sooner turn than return. And can't we
        not praise our now perfect bodies, raise our faces
to show we have real eyes, try our own slow
        hand at it, whenever the red, just, right, tight,
time, spreads, thin, clean, line, points,
        out, what's, new, a, head, today, and, on,
and, on, and, on, and, on, and, on, and,
        on, and, on, and, on, and, on, and, on.

The Beginning of the Last Fall

Not the last, long August of your fast, short life,
perhaps not. But not the shut-door, take-home, quick-
fix talk of the lack of summer's auguries.
Not the knock-kneed kids at the goal post nor
the CD played out nor lips unfastened with
kisses nor dishes becoming porcelain
again. Neither the ether to kill
the cecropia moth nor the belief
that its resurrection on a wall will
save something else nor the knowledge of
the one hundred feet from the one hundred
foot ledge is enough. You need not know
about the auroras you missed, the halos, nor
the wild wet burst of air that will pull the leaves down.

Speed of Life

Your heart is over. You do things the hard
    way. You dream you are still scrubbing the paint
off your hands from the factory. And then the facts
    pile up: the voice box closed tight, the spine
like the curve in the road you always dream
    you run off, brain boiling in its membrane.
If you could guess at life, life's crests,
    you still can't stop the flood waters from
washing away every sandbag you've ever imagined.
    When your plane leaves tomorrow, it will crash.
You've had time to think. What was thought?
    What is the color of your death? The green,
yellow, red of the traffic lights, the aquamarine
    of the water now ten feet of it covering you,
the white knifeblade sliding into your lungs?
    Cry the cry. Play dead. Take down the mosquito
netting over your deathbed. You dream
    of floating in a long wooden boat, two thick
wax candles stuck in your eyes. You didn't see
    the saw spinning toward you, cutting you in two.
Time's too short for the long division. Add,
    add, add. Take away, take away, take away.
You hear yourself cough up a syllable of doubt
    in a sentence of belief. Neither makes your
life longer or shorter. You dream that you have
    become an hour and that there are twenty-four
of you in a day. You think, Was that backfire
    or gun shot? The fire on the hillside was
only one hundred yards away. You've travelled
    fast in the past, now faster, breaking apart,
losing the last small error of control you thought
    was locked inside you forever, you thought
was beyond the everything that is now gone.

· Two ·

Abortion

For crying out loud, she was shot.
The pitcher continued to throw, even though
everyone else was on strike. Everybody
I know has had one and everybody
I know hasn't. They tossed their cookies
on the Tilt-a-Whirl. Ever been thrown out
of a game, for swinging on the rim, for
roughing up the kicker? When they
looked in the mirror, they saw homunculi
everywhere. In the distance, nickels and quarters
spinning a racket in the dryers. Help is a
far cry. Eject me, Lord, for it is a cruel
and unusual world. How can you not be
troubled by doom, doom, doom. If one foot
is in the coffin, pray tell, where then would
the other foot be? O shoe, please drop.
And then I erased so hard I left
this enormous hole in the middle of the page!

Alcohol and Drug Abuse

Today I want to talk about the future
of alcohol and drug abuse. Could you
listen up? The dried Greek figs I bought
yesterday were strung on a string like ears?
Will they be eaten? Who is listening?
Alcohol is a fine powder of antinomy used
to tint the eyelids. Will the statues in
the garden ever truly blink? And *drug* is
the nonstandard past tense of *drag, will
have drug*, for example. Will the drudgery
of chores finally evolve into a happiness
with ordinary actions? These are the questions
before us. Let us be quick to consider their
answers. At what point does the wet nurse give
way to the dry nurse, then to no nurse, then to
us doing the nursing? There will be a time
when all the sutures will be sewn shut. If we
won't be there to see it, we are still in the present
of present—the last great gift we can never use up.

Capital Punishment

It's time for a little bifurcation followed by a little
up yours. O how death goes on and on at the mouth,
eternal balloons in the clogged arteries. Such
a lethal conjecture we entertain. Cut off the balls
of all the baby boys, while you're at it. The dead
bodies roll so messily into the mass graves.
Let's watch 'em fry! Turn me over, I think
I'm done on this side, said the grillee to the griller.
N👁④N👁: punish me in lower-case. What a gas it was
when we spent the day tattooing hieroglyphs on our biceps,
the ibis wiggling when we flexed. A little life penalty never
hurt. We should maim them not kill them—suck out all
their muscle with a straw. Break their teeth with big rocks.
Paint them blue. Arrange for roses to grow out of their ears.
Death is the fastest rower in the slowest boat.

Child Abuse

The death rattle held in the small sticky hand
of the baby faking crib death or is its blue baby
blanket stuffed in its mouth, cheeks
bulging like big water-filled blisters
we would want to slice open? Or
fucked to death, shot to death, shot
by death, fucked by death. Don't
hand us that shit about diaper rash.
Trash the baby and the baby becomes
trash. Ask it to behave itself around
adult bodies. It squirms like a
larva in the bathwater. We're bored
with it, its blue wailing, its constant
chubbiness, its fingernails the size
of lice, its senseless innocence. Tie
it to the back of a wolf. Watch it tumble
in the dryer. Burn off its fingerprints.
Send it down the laundry chute. Whip
it until the whip breaks. Sharpen
the bayonet it got for Christmas. Gag
it. Make it talk. Rub red pepper on its
gums. Roll it in flour before baking.
Baste it in its own juices. Listen to
it squeak and spit up. Listen to it coo
the most ridiculous coos. Listen to it
die, after having swallowed the last of
five million gulps of air, after having heard
jars of baby food smashing against the walls,
after seeing who killed it, seeing who gave it life.

The End of Fascism, Nazism, Communism, Capitalism

Nobody owns us. We've stood on street corners
with our charred scorecards and we know
the village villains, their curved knives that cut
our purse strings. Or it's pow, pow, pow,
pow, pow, pow, power: unload a barrel
of bullets into us and watch us abandon
our flesh and our blood. Divide our bodies
among the hog futures. This is all you think
of us. But totalitarianism isn't a toss-up.
Feeling a little giddy at the guillotine? Mind
you, when you phone us, press 1 for ruthless
oppression, 2 for absolute power, 3 for elimination
of all opposition, or stay on the line. However,
we're either away from our desk or we're on
another line. But we will FedEx hate to your bunkers,
we will deposit your bankers in the holds of your
yachts, we will lug your thugs by their ears, we
will roadblock your moneybags, make you gag
on power until it comes out of your nose, give
you a face then deface you, nothing, absolutely
nothing is too good for you. Hate is the high
hat you wore. It was the easiest thing in the world
to knock it off your head.

Euthanasia

Allow no law to limit the choosing of our brief moment
of dying. Someone simply bumps the car: the car's alarm
goes off: then silence. Slice open your tendinous wrists
and call it suicide, the last long slow slide. Allow
that there be a good death but not a great death.
But allow us to die, and allow us the means to that end.
Overheard in the hospital ward last week: I'd love to pull
your plug. I'd love to plug you in. Turn the key and turn
the alarm off and drive away. Winch out the four-stroke
engine of the body. That it could swing from heavy chains
in the garage forever! Braid the rows of daffodils
after they've bloomed. I've been a witness to the good
health of dying: one lovely unstockinged bright
good foot in the grave. Incipient irises are
positioned to grow in the topsoil, pushing themselves
up from their fat selves-as-bulbs, selves
we don't see, selves we thought all this time were dead.

Nuclear War

If thy itchy trigger finger offend thee, slice it
off; burn it; or tie it—you attached—to the bumper
of rapid transit, and be dragged eternally around
town. War is neither very new nor very
clear. Smash the bottle of God. Spill
the elixir of health. Just leave me
out of it—I want to peel onion after onion
and watch myself cry. What is the *it* that was
over before we knew it? We were bored: we
pushed each other's buttons. Irradiate me, Lord,
for I am singed. (Live) boys will be (dead) boys.
Aftermath: biology, literature, religion. As someone
famous said: war is raw. This is not a test. All
the generals clear their throats, discreetly pocket
their balls. Pretty scary, pretty scary, pretty scary,
pretty scary, pretty scary, pretty scary, pretty scary.

Politico-Religious Syllogisms

The Religious Right are wrong, the Religious Wrong
are right, the Religious Right are left, the Religious
Left are right, therefore the Religious North are green,
the Religious Red are blue, the Religious Lite are
dark, the Religious Blue are fat, the Religious Fat
are here, the Religious Dark are dead, the Religious
Dead are right, the Religious Right are dead, the Religious
Sons are set, therefore the Religious Cars are black,
the Religious Black are wet, the Religious White are
right, the Religious Poor are dour, therefore the Religious
Rich are kitsch, the Religious Just are cussed, the Religious
Cows are milked, the Religious Rugs are washed,
the Religious Trucks are crashed, the Religious Nights
are bright, the Religious Bucks are shot, the Religious
Kids are poor, the Religious Poor are dead, therefore
the Religious Kites are down, the Religious Stocks are
up, the Religious Bonds are down, the Religious Dikes
are built, the Religious Pacs are wrong, the Religious
Right are wrong, the Religious Right are wrong,
therefore, the Religious Right are wrong.

Violence

It's a skill you learned: The hatchet job
on the corpse in the closed coffin,
the crybaby in the burned out crib,

the hair in your hand you've pulled out
from someone's head. Practice your tricks
in the knot garden with human beings

who have turned into human nothings,
groups of are-nots. Not that you believe
shame is a shim to make the door frame square.

You walked out that door long ago. You
slid down the blood-covered steps. You
blood-let with the best. You collected eye-

balls and index fingers. You invented the hissed *s*
of slaughter. Could you not cuddle your guns for once?
Could you not spray sperm in all directions

for once? Ask the children you've done in—
The solace of the barbwire fence, the comfort
of the jungle gym decorated with dead kids—

birth is the party Death threw and screwed everyone,
including you. Hang yourself. Cut your throat.
(Do what you need to do.) Drown. Crash your

car. (Say so long to brief time!) Jump off
the bridges. Push the trigger with your big
toe. (Enjoy the long fall.) Slice yourself

into the smallest possible pieces. Ignite.
Scatter your own ashes. You have done it.
You are as dead as anyone you have ever killed.

Racism, Classism, Sexism

The big boys played all day with their isms.
Then they smashed poems made in their own
likenesses. Then they divided their earned
run averages by the difference between stop
and go, and then they slept for forty days and
forty nights. Then they peppered the blue sky
with bird shot. Then all the leaves on the trees
turned into money for them. Then the war, then
more war, then more and more. Then the happiness
from twelve to twelve-thirty. Then big tears.
Then everybody died and then they just thought
they died. And then they said let's start over and
then they chose sides, and then those sides
chose sides, chose sides, chose sides. And then
those sides chose sides, and those sides chose
sides, and then those sides chose sides.

A Bad God

Got guts in his rucksack, carries
them home for dinner.
                            No knife and
fork folk, no. Eats with his hand

that he holds his pisser with. O how we
tumbled after winning the three-legged
race, my brother and I,
                            fucked over by
factory life. We were God snot. We

were God spit and God shit.
                          When every
speck of life we've had in jars turns,
lock all the children in refrigerators and

let them die. Seal the doors with the wax
from God ears.
                      Yes, strafed by the Bad God—
there is no hope left that more hope
                                 can handle.

O slick shiny blood! Swell these artless arteries
and make them burst. The want of
                            death to grind
our lenses. We want to see the man in the coffin

sawn in two. We want to see the Bad God face close
up so we can remember it
                      as we scour it off every wall.

War

Scarcely have I written a word and the world
is lost to me. Like taking someone away from
someone, giving that someone to someone else.
There is one sun to see each morning. I want
the most words to go to those who have
the least words, fewer than the fingers
on both hands. The only way to walk
around this stupid battlefield
is with all our pockets turned inside out:
Show the bloodred linings of our hearts,
show that our souls need replastering.
Show that our eyes are sick in their
sockets, that our mouths have evaporated
like the water in the glasses we can't drink from.
O Words of Abundance! Scatter
those you love to those you hate. Make
all the branches of all the trees in this world equal.
Better to love than not to love, to love than not to love.
Better to love than not to love, to love than not to love.

Welfare Reform

Behold the teenage mother-to-be with an attitude!
Hail to thee. Fare thee well. May the bubble
in your belly become the baby that becomes
the best poet of all time. May this baby become
well-read, well-fixed, well-meaning. May this baby
become well-fed, well-mannered, welcome. May
this baby become well-groomed, well-grounded,
well-known. I have seen the well-to-do who do
and I have seen the well-to-do who don't. I too
have spoken with the women at the well, and I too
have heard the timbre of good cheer throughout
the land. Might that we'll all be well-born. Might
that the horn of plenty replenish those punished, those
in plight. Might that the day's work of the well-
intentioned be love. Might that well-being be.

· Three ·

To Remain

November sixteenth, nineteen-eighty-nine,
In San Salvador, the unsaved city,
The soldiers rephrase *Genesis*: Let there be

Light, so we can see those we're killing,
The right bodies or the wrong bodies.
The death squad posters say, *Be a Patriot,*

Kill a Priest. And on this night the Atlacatl
Battalion, accents of training drills at Fort
Benning, Georgia, still in their ears, *Made*

In the U. S. A. bullets in their belts, circle
The University of Central America. Inside the gates,
They drag five Jesuits from their cots, men who

Yesterday said masses for the massacred, their
Minds now reminded of no new future testament.
They are now face down, fatherly eyes in the dust

Of the courtyard. And according to the official
Report, the bodies are lined from north to south,
With their heads toward the west, and their feet

Stretched toward the east. And after the killing,
After the commander's simple words, "Let's proceed,"
There remains Amando López, 55, theology professor,

Found in the following position: head to the west,
Feet pointed to the east, mouth down, left arm bent
Toward the west, right arm bent to the east, dressed

In striped shorts, green poncho, green jeans. And easily
Found next to him, there remains Ignacio Martín Baró, 46,
Psychology professor and Vice-Rector, found in

The following position: head to the west, feet
To the east, left arm to the west, right arm bent
To the north, right foot on the left foot, mouth

Down, wearing a blue shirt, black leather belt, gray
Pants, black shoes and socks. And Segundo Montes, 56,
Sociology professor and Director of Human Rights, who

Had said, "I want to live with the people who suffer
And deserve more," found in the following position:
Mouth down, feet extended to the northeast, head

To the southwest, left arm and right arm bent
Below the head with direction to the south,
Wearing beige shorts, beige shirt, and green jeans.

And next to him, Ignacio Ellacuría, 59,
University Rector, mouth down, head to the north,
Feet to the south, left arm to the north, right

Arm bent toward the face, wearing a brown bathrobe,
Beige shorts with vertical stripes, blue shoes. And
Next to him Juan Ramón Moreno, 55, theology professor,

Found in the following position: mouth down, head
To the east, feet to the west, arms extended toward
The southwest, dressed in black corduroy pants, black

Belt, long-sleeved blue shirt, purple shorts, brown
Leather shoe on the right foot. And inside
The residence, one remaining priest, called Lolo,

Joaquin López y López, 71, Director of *Fé y Alegría*,
The quiet one, who was chased through the corridors,
Found in the following position: mouth up, head

To the east, feet to the west, arms bent over
The chest, hands semi-closed, wearing a white sleeveless
Undershirt, brown pants, black belt, shorts with vertical

Stripes. And in the room off the kitchen, where they asked
To spend the night to escape the night of city violence,
Of quiet killings done quickly, the new siege, civilians

Beholding that one brightest star exploding, as their
Roofs are torn off by bombs, children watching
Fire fights after curfew through cracks in the walls,

In this room, Elba Julia Ramos, 40, Jesuit Community cook,
Mouth up, head to the north, left foot to the south and right
Foot to the southwest, right arm to the northwest, left arm

To the southeast, both extended, wearing a blue dress, beige
Slip, black leather shoes, white bra; and her daughter,
Celina Ramos, 15, high school student, mouth up, head to

The north, feet to the south, right arm over the chest, left arm
Perpendicular to the left side with direction to the north,
Wearing blue shorts, black, orange, red, and beige vertically

Striped blouse, white leather shoes with laces. Elba and Celina,
Who were "rekilled" when heard moaning from wounds, were
Found embracing before the M-16 fired ten more bullets

Into their bodies. And Elba was discovered that morning
By her husband at the same moment that Celina was discovered
That morning by her father, a *campesino* who cannot

Write this down, but instead weeks later planted two white rose
Bushes in the courtyard, one for Elba, one for Celina,
And surrounded them with six red rose bushes, one to the north,

One to the south, one to the east, one to the west, cardinal
Points, and two to directions that haven't been invented yet,
A compass of roses that searches for where we are going,

That can tell us where we have been. The white bushes
Are like the needle in the compass that tries to point
Beyond compassion. Or to tell us who the third person left

Standing is, the one who sees all, the witness, the one
Who has testimony, who has lamentation, who stands in
For the 70,000 Salvadorans killed in one decade.

· Four ·

Blood Bank

The click of the counter in the turnstile
woke me up out of that dream I have while
walking: the war between the heels and

soles of my shoes. I had stopped at the blood
bank earlier to make a deposit and still feel
subcutaneous, the false euphoria of sugared

doughnuts dropping like the downramp in
the parking garage. A fleet of bloodmobiles
in the side lot is dunked red, the cots

inside still hot. My car clock has stopped
in nearly the exact spot as my father's car
clock, a quarter to four, whether a.m. or p.m.

I don't know. My eyes are bloodshot in
the mirror on the underside of the visor. On his,
my father has six plastic drops of blood, one

for each gallon he has given. He believed
in bloodletting and now his blood pressure is
higher than the bell ringing at the carnival,

hit hard with the shot from the mallet.
He hasn't won prizes. He eats less red meat,
although he grew up on *czernina*, soup

thickened with duck's blood, and has got
a blood count that won't quit. I'd rather
be driving away from the blood bank than

driving toward the blood shed, where
my brother worked for four summers, squeegeeing
turkey blood into a hole in the middle of

the floor. He got paid in bloodmoney.
He was called a bloodsucker. He is at
the end of his bloodline, is holding on so

hard that his hands are white. I have lain
on the table with a tube in my arm, watched
the plastic sack fill up with drops, fill

out with a thickness that is always viscous
inside me, the art of the artery, veins
of gold, struck, bleeding colors, split and splitting.

Brisance

for Tamara Verga, 1970-1990

We are still trying to turn the doorknob on the back porch
of the smoke-filled house, choked thoughts of dark, fresh
air outside, opened books of poems by the sofa on
which you fell asleep. Picture something other than:
not unwrapping the package of death, not crashing
through the car window at eighty miles-per-hour, not falling
in the wells that don't exist. If we've never believed
weather reports or traffic reports, we don't intend
to start now. *Now* is its own wound—what came before
was really what was going to happen, this
opening up so you can die, closed up tightly
forever, the last thrill of drilling deep into earth,
some spiral of memory, somehow remembering
a way back down the ladder you reluctantly climbed.
You've lost your footing, and the pears stay overripe at the very
top of the tree. But how to get them down when the tree
grows so high? *Nothing* is easy. It's the *something*
we have a hard time making happen. You had not been
building a twenty-year-old coffin. You didn't give
wood and nails the gravity they wanted. The sad nest
the cats tore apart is covered with snow. Perhaps only
the dead see the brilliant light the living make when
they die. A poem's white page is torn in two. What is
the rate at which we separate from this life? You,
lying on the floor, dead. You, sitting in the chair, alive.

Century

It so happens my hundredth birthday falls
on the last Sunday in October 2051. And if

I am not there to mark that day: might
someone add three drops of river water

to my ashes, pound them with a pestle,
pour them in a mold. The more I bid

to buy the cost of living this life,
the less is left to take in some last

cardboard suitcase. I will be over-
taken, then undertaken, but now I don't

need a mirror held up to my mouth,
fogged up with breath or not. One

hundred years ago I was less than a *centesimo*,
the face on that coin long rubbed away.

Can we keep from jumping off the ledge
of the next century? My father uses

the handrail that at eighty he inherited.
Long live his new wood cane. He taps

out Greek hexameters like
Sophocles.

       O long memory!
can't I not now die with you!

Humiliation

It was summer, 1963, when Roman Borzyskowski's
   fifth-grade wiener transformed into some eighth
      grade hard-on right there, at the Lake Winona beach

in front of Febronia Bublitz, Viola Papenfuss, Sylvia
   Orzechowski, all of us. It was sticking out of the top
      of his St. Vincent de Paul swimsuit like the red

top of a plastic bobber, the kind at the end of every fine
   fishing line of every cane pole down at The Gut, where
      the Swift's meat-packing plant dumped what they couldn't

use, and the carp swirled. And the tenth-grade boys,
   always alert to public erections, grabbed him around
      the chest, pulled down those blue shorts like peeling off

a beer bottle label, and two of them hauled him around
   the grass by his legs, his hard thing like some spring
      uncoiled, or like the antenna on the hood

of my Uncle Syl's 1950 Chevy, picking
   up broadcasts from as far away as Witoka,
      the polkas, the Chester Cichosz Farm Report.

Roman had a green ass when they were through
   with that moment's description of fun, his
      hard-on flicked off to a thin thumb-shaped,

circumcised, normal, and now humiliated
   thing. We had not suspected Kennedy would be
      killed soon, or that it would happen so

graphically, so publicly, the image singeing
    our eyes. Think of his live wife, spattered
        with blood. We kept up the card game, penny

poker, Lucky Strikes for the ante, half-naked
    women wearing out on the backs of every ace,
        every deuce, every king. The lucky won.

The unlucky had their very first hard-ons exposed
    to the world. What was the matter with us
        that matter couldn't manage to change? Roman

brushed sand off his elbow. It was over now.
    He ran his shorts back up his body like a flag,
        simply like a flag.

Equal Sign

The sutures close the cut face, wrong rungs on the rope
ladder, crisscrosses. Who coined death? Have we become
the home bodies who refuse to house souls?
Where are gut buckets now that we need them?
On wash day I heard the women singing, to the scrub board,
the wash pan, black water spilling over the sides.
O, I have knelt on the sidewalk to retie my shoelace,
and then thought of my young grandmother picking apart
the flour sacks to make curtains for Easter and her husband's
father ripping them down. They were not plain enough.
They had embroidery. I think of the morning we sat
polishing our lens of silence. When she died I thought
this was the end of *and*, and I was wrong. There were words
at the bottom of the sack, enough to put up a wall of talk.
In the weathered barn, a squall of pigs. Chickens in,
chickens out. Horse neighs. Yes, it's the truth. Motion
is local. I've felt entropy when I've entered the trophy
store, feeling as if I should order plaques for my failures.
Is a rose *greater than* a bird's wing? My grandmother had *This
is the first night of the rest of your death* handwritten in
her Bible. I remember eating the cake she won at the cakewalk,
and it was like any other cake. She made soap out of ashes
and fat. Who do we turn to in catastrophe? We are all
equal at the four-way stop. I love the rings around
the bull's eye, the continuous orbit, in contrast to the linear
obituary, the mortician chopping off your ring finger.
I hope I've written my last dead letter. We queue up
to see that which equalizes: one summer left or fifty, entry level
or overtime. Early warning system or not, we'll be getting there.

Preoccupation

I rode my bicycle to work all the fall of 1974, lunch pail
snapped in the back rack. I was busily out of college,
out of money, taken over by the feeling that if two wheels,
thin and wiry, can carry me over long sets of railroad tracks
to the paint factory, then I will always get there, forever
arrive under the fifty-foot can of paint, tipped, out of
which flows neon-lit paint. All day on the
mainline, I clipped on the ear protectors because
the ten thousand empty gallon cans filing by clashed like
oblivion. Sound was its own fixative, and then the
four seconds under the nozzle that filled the can,
the lid pressed on by a roller, the handle twisted on,
the can boxed, the boxes taped, the boxes stacked on
pallets, the pallets loaded on the dock, the stacked
pallets loaded onto trucks, then driven somewhere, unloaded,
the cans put on shelves, the can bought and taken home,
opened, brush dipped in, paint slapped on walls.
I was part of the progress I didn't want any part in,
the year Nixon resigned, giving that stiff wave on the helicopter
platform, leaving work in the way we were all leaving
it each day, some guttural *Fuck you* behind that smile
of knowing we're done for the moment and, if we don't die
in the night, will be back at seven the next morning,
worried about seeing out the next eight hours. I was
laid off, but was hired the following week at another factory,
made all the yellow center line for Minnesota, Wisconsin,
Iowa, and North and South Dakota. Heavy lead paint
I still can't wash off. It was good training to become
a terrorist. When you're in the state of being held,
you want to repossess what you have most loved,
what you didn't know, what you were about to find out.

Seizure

I remember the mason jar of pennies near the fuse box,
   the power lines, frozen in the ice storm, feeding
      into the house. We would catch coffee at the *Sturm und*

Drang, pour down potfuls, hoping to unclog the brain
   drain. Ah, we thought of real closure, of things actually
      closing, the convenience store at midnight, the selfserve

car wash with the world's most powerful vacuum. When I turn
   over the closed sign, I'm gone, eyesight a tight suture
      to what I see. I've dreamed of being born in a corn crib,

swaddling clothes and all, but I wake up on my way
   to the eight grain elevators I'm helping to build, pushing
      a buggy of concrete, dumping it into forms. We rise

each shift three feet. It's my adventure, I can see
   myself saying, puncturing the speech balloon floating
      above my head. Because I could not start my car, I took

the bus instead. During the accident, everyone will tell
   you, everything happened so fast. I heard a buzz saw
      when I died I heard myself saying. The photographs

in court were grainy. Everyone was so cocksure of their
   point of view, thermometers in the cold ovens. Instead
      of clipping the weeds around literature, my grandmother

hoed the rhubarb. She was the one who tied the lure
   on my fishing line. Destroy Troy and you get Thermopylae,
      she always said, the allure of the ransack, the diamond

on the uninsured finger. I've heard hysteria runs
   in the family, and there's no cure, not even acupuncture
      helps. And all the while I wanted to conjugate spring,

conjure it, assure myself of rapture. If I seek to know,
   where's pleasure? Fire catching the big logs after
      crackling the newspaper, heat in the earth again, erasing

whiteness, the freeing of those green shoots that we had
   all thought had lost any further gesture, were unable
      to go past an earth seized up from the pressure of winter?

Rapid Fire

In the photograph of our seventh grade basketball
team at St. Stanislaus, I am standing next to

Bruce Pomeroy, who did not die six years later
in Vietnam but in a car crash one year after

returning. He had been on his way out. He had
done most of the common *spires*, from *as* to *per* to

re, and his run on the spiral ran down. The second
hand on the watch he had been wearing went around

and around, like his father on the construction site
tamping the steaming asphalt, giving the road a

surface we often walk upon. There's not enough
of Bruce Pomeroy now to say much. He was a random

variable, a last stat on the late news. He was taken
away by a fleet of flying saucers, something like

the kind he used to shoot at on Saturday mornings.
His mother's tavern was the last place I got

blind-drunk. The war was just a parabola to us
then, something thrown aside, some backpack abandoned

in a place we knew we'd never return to. Bruce Pomeroy
didn't read the dictionary so didn't know there are

three pages of words beginning with *self*. This wouldn't
have helped his self-esteem. We had been on some kind

of verge. It was night. We had been working all
day as arc welders. When his car broke through

the ice as he was spinning away from the car
he was racing, that I was driving, he had had

the windows open, and the Mississippi River simply
closed up over him. We had both been shifting

into fourth gear, at least. Now that some of that water
has gone underground, a river Styx rubbing

the faces off stones, I think that the only racing
in an iced-over river I've done is done. Every

five years the river is dredged for channel,
a chance that someone will go continually downstream.

The Rent

I've slept under freeway overpasses long before the crumbling
infrastructure talk of today. I would walk down the ram's horn
ramp and, warm in my down bag, would count the cars until

I fell asleep. As some of you may know, some of us may not.
I thought my father invented the split decision, but it was
really the division of labor, one hundred under one, and he

happened not to be the one. He taught me how to hold
the stick to stir my brain each morning, like a bucket
of white paint left uncovered overnight, thin white skin

floating on it. Did whoever first wanted to split the atom
do so out of disagreement? It's not always those in uniform
that arrest your development. Neighbors kept a temporary gar

in their garden pond. They liked to slap around a black puck
of hate. It was the early seventies, off-center times, Watergate,
Nixon was that thing on the water, that island, as oily

as Exxon. I'm happy to surrender tradition if it's all about
traitors. My wristwatch of that time has rusted. And Reagan
has long gone fishing for quiddities. His figure of speech

was a pile of weeds, a rhapsody of worms, rancid butter,
a donut nation. I know that the window is what
the wind knows will keep it out, a union of glass

and wood, transparent time, the right song punched
on the jukebox, but the wrong sound. No one's ever
asked me if I've had my feet bound, but I remember my

uncle's feet splitting open with gangrene. I imagined his
wooden leg was a large pencil, and that he scraped
a hieroglyph of his pain on the sidewalk. He wrote out

his rendition of sorrow, beginning with the rows of corn
he would sow, the stalks of time he would then cut.
He got on at the last stagestop. I was of an age,

different from carnage or dotage, the montage
of marriage, some washed-out time, gouached now, a flicker
of the beeper telling me I've a call, and can take it on

the cellular phone. Something, by inference, seems warped,
some rapid twisting, like wringing out the white from the sheets
until there is nothing left at all. But the faucet's always

there, certainly a vending machine nearby too, and if there is
wrong doing, then there is right doing. You don't need a car
in order to drive, you can neither buy nor rent, and you can

certainly stay for any reason under the overpass: perhaps
you took the same road, the straight not the curved,
the tarred not the dirt, the short not the long, the wrong.

Worry

Old E.J. is losing it. I see him talking
to his sisters through the transistor radio
held up to his ear. They have been dead
for as long as the rain clears the streets
of all memory we have of them. He's
been seized by the throat but doesn't
know it to talk about it. He's hoary
with worry that the snow won't cover all
of him, that his face will be the right food
for field mice. He looks at the black
crows crow white words. His walker
walks without him. No more thoughts
about how warm his grandfather's hands
would be on the trapeze bars in the German
circus. No more thoughts of his last nine
words to me, "And say hi to Eddie when
you see him." I saw him in the mirror this
morning, shaving, razor stropped and poised
an inch below the deep gashes, his
neck slashed years ago, old folded
skin now covering the scars. I remember
feeling the thick cords, can hear the words
that are continuously stuck in some guttural
and mysterious speech. He doesn't recognize
my voice, my soon-to-be-dead father—
words clear over phone lines, lines tied
to each of us, tugging and stretching,
until we can't remember hearing them break.

Subito

My father tells me he wants to go quickly: in the midst
    of tipping the bottle back, while completing the U-turn,
after defrosting the turkey in the kitchen sink. He'd
    rather not linger, Death's finger pointing him out in
the line at the post office, and he'd have to wait
    for hours to reach the front. The wick burns where
the flame is. He wishes that his watch would
    start its alarm, slice open his left wrist, and do
a quick countdown, but he knows that his body's
    business is to manage to breathe, and it would flood
the market with self-preservation. My father has had
    a shelf life of eighty years. He's the bottle in
the cellar given half-turns every six months. He's had
    a leg crushed, a lung collapse, and a face smashed.
His feet curl up in the fire he has imagined starting
    in himself, using what he reads each night, *The Joy*
of Death, for kindling. He's split up his insect
    collection, and now it's worthless. Only his
footprints are the signs that he's going. He wants
    a big truck to break through the gates of hell. He carries
a body bag in the glove compartment, an effigy of
    himself in the trunk. He has turned health into death,
every breath is gunning the engine, watching the fuel
    gauge feel itself go empty. It's his age, the nightshade
he sprinkles in his teacup, the way he can twang a string,
    and the vibration is enough to send the undertaker over,
pulling a trailer of coffins, and a word processor full
    of sample eulogies. My father rides the nightmare to
the farm he lost, the farm that burned down, a big
    sickle slicing the wheat of his memory. If it were
done, it were to be done quickly, the big quit of life,
    the heart attack at the front line, no defensive action,
no camouflage, flak jacket, no bandages, no pain
    pills, no interruption from the sweet swift act of death.

EDWARD KLEINSCHMIDT MAYES'S books of poetry include *First Language* (Juniper Prize), *To Remain* (Gesù Award), and *Magnetism* (Poetry Award from Bay Area Book Reviewers Association). His poems have appeared in *American Poetry Review, Gettysburg Review, Iowa Review, Massachusetts Review, New England Review, New Yorker, Poetry, TriQuarterly, Virginia Quarterly Review,* and *Best American Poetry*. He received a 1997 National Endowment for the Arts Fellowship in Poetry. A collection of his love poems, *Bodysong,* was published this year by The Heyeck Press. *Works and Days* (Associated Writing Programs Award Series), an abecedarius of poems about Italy, will be published by University of Pittsburgh Press this fall. He is Director of the Creative Writing Program at Santa Clara University and lives in San Francisco and Cortona, Italy, with the writer Frances Mayes.